D1104892

Confidence

Confidence

Seth Landman

Brooklyn Arts Press · New York

Confidence
© 2015 Seth Landman

ISBN-13: 978-1-936767-39-7

Cover art by Bovey Lee. Cover design by Joe Pan. Interior design by Ben DuVall. Edited by Broc Rossell. Marketed by Sam Hall.

Published in the United States of America by:
Brooklyn Arts Press
154 N 9th St #1
Brooklyn, NY 11249
www.BROOKLYNARTSPRESS.COM
INFO@BROOKLYNARTSPRESS.COM

Distributed to the trade by Small Press Distribution / SPD
www.spdbooks.org

LIBRARY OF CONGRESS CATALOGING-IN-PUBLICATION DATA

LANDMAN, SETH, 1982-
[POEMS. SELECTIONS]
CONFIDENCE / SETH LANDMAN.
     PAGES ; CM
ISBN 978-1-936767-39-7 (PBK. : ALK. PAPER)
I. TITLE.

PS3612.A548355A6 2014
811'.6--DC23
                              2014019663

10 9 8 7 6 5 4 3 2 1
FIRST EDITION

Contents

This is the most the book-maker can attain to.
If he make his volume a mole whereon the waves
of Silence may break, it is well.

—Henry David Thoreau, *A Week on the Concord
and Merrimack Rivers*

Telling You I Love You

I love the feeling
I cut myself off
I let on I know light
like the back of my hand
but I don't
know or see
the end of this
mystery

I love the feeling
the blood bank
I can't walk myself home
one person walking
past everything
life is
a movie
I'm deceived by the jargon
your face

I love the feeling
the wind is a song
the wind is a song
I love the feeling
without knowing anything
I'd rather be
you in my hoodie

I love the feeling
I let the light
know the lack a little
sometimes I write
for you
the look on your face
I don't know
how it makes you feel
I don't know how it makes you feel

I love the wind
and the song
is the feeling
it's not accurate
but this feels good
like a good time
like a good time to go
so far away

I love to think I could know
what the wind feels
all these voices and shapes
and the good shapes your body takes
as the wind goes
and sounds around it
I run through them remembering
hoping the light
from my phone
is you again

I love fresh water
monsters
or at least I prefer them
and small houses

and things I can keep
in narrow focus
on good nights
in September
I prefer them turning
the light on under the lake

I love clarifications
the energy of talking
getting upset
spinning out of control
I love saying love
not even meaning it
but yes meaning it also
just saying the next thing
uncertain breeziness
just telling you what I'm gonna do
and doing it

I love the wind
and the song
and the feeling
and the meaning
and the red way
dreams have
of watching movies
I mean I love the movies
concessions
whispers
confidences
and hands
mouths and secrets
making out

I love all this
doubt and religion
my arm around you
here is the cosmos
here are the sizes
I love all this doubt
in the shape
of opinion
with the sun going down
and one light blinking
across the sky
swept up by sweet impulse
by fear sometimes
you can get in order
sometimes you think
of the universe
like sizes
of popcorn
fries or soda
the universe small
medium large
extra large
extra extra large
extra extra extra large

I love astronomy
a constellation
you see yourself in the stars
at the edge of the field
low in the sky
over the trees
I'm telling you I love
to focus on attrition
like lower back pain

or repeating a word
alone in the car
until it's gone
or the decision a cloud makes to rain
to change my mind

I love to not feel anything
but not for too long
in my extremities
my mouth
sometimes won't shut up
when I'm drinking whiskey
I love justifying
behavior saying this right here
is cause for celebration
there's a bonfire
everyone is around it
everything is ridiculous
now picture a fire talking
kicking and screaming
whatever you want
it's funny
the fire loves you
it's pretty hot
don't touch it
it loves you
you're going out

I love Mount Everest
I've never been there
but I love it
and keep going
put your head
on my shoulder

hold me in the twin bed
in the bedroom
that was mine
keep going
spoon me under the panorama
of the old Boston Garden
reach under the rubble
for souvenirs
because it's impossible
to know what you'll care about
and returning
to Mount Everest
in all your travels
you won't go there
how little you
don't reveal

I love history
it's hard to say why
I love the small kinds of saying
little performances
for how many years
and some other variables
and let this particular unknown stand
for what I am afraid to admit
to myself tonight
and what has been carefully registered
and you have to admit
there's luck involved
and I love luck
I thought of it
as my life
fudging numbers
I invented this

idea of myself
but I don't know
will history be kind

I love these photographs
of the world
before I got here
when my folks
in their youth
had yet to imagine my life
or getting older
I love that world
in dusty color
and standard definition
I'm trying to remember
as you have to remember
to love what you invented
the fundamental
songs stuck in your head
will always welcome you
oh and one more thing
before you go

I love one more thing
one more time
one more day
one more chance
and another one
late at night
with a little buzz going
the long moments
after you've said how you feel
to the voice
paused on the other end

anything is possible
I love the end of the day
anything after
long moments
I'm staying up
for the fundamental
things in the world
gravity
and gravity around you
I love one
and one
and one
welcoming one to another
I love what a friend says
and how a friend says it
the judgment of the night itself
with no response
just saying I've been thinking about you
in long moments
I thought and I thought
and now I'm thinking

I love you
and I haven't told you yet
it's sad to be loved
on the huge grid
that's life
it's passing
you in the street
at the right moment
it's sad to be loved
with little in return
it's sad
not to love someone

in return
you must retrieve it
and there's no chance
and all the green money
doesn't do it
you can't just jump
off a cliff
I'm sorry I don't love this person
when in return
you don't love me
it's a sad equation
I haven't told you
I'm just assuming
it's sad
I love you

I love what I thought you meant
and what you actually meant
I worry about
types of boundaries
trees on the fields' edge
the limit of what we can see
the curvature of the earth
from an airplane window
and history
another love song
I should love into the night
driving through Oklahoma City
to Boston
from San Francisco
how much time lived
as opposed to how much time left
years later
you love

Oklahoma City
you think about
places left and about
places still uncovered
talk to yourself
in the car
in total confidence
you're worrying
about another
driving
love

I love feeling I'm lost
a man in a forest
a drop of rain
falling exactly ambivalently onto the apex
of the continental divide of the continent where
I've been living
a raindrop
who knows
about other parts of the world
a little about their particular watersheds
just a droplet
a great research
I love feeling
in a forest
the pinch of an insect
a tap on the shoulder
and no one is there
in quiet
winter
you have walked
into being alone
in the forest everything's clear

I love being
watched by the animals
but people are animals
but not by the people
but by the other animals
the people I know
some of them
even fewer
no fewer
no fewer
fewer
that's it
right there
I love the ambivalent division
of water inside
our bodies falling exactly as we've been living
and there's no planning for it
the decision's been made
the feeling in the forest
but I'm not
in the falling
I'm right there
in the way
of the water

I love this evening
the phrase itself
maybe a slight chill
this evening
in the cool air
on a porch
with a whiskey
this evening
an impressive sky

and my bad habits easing off
and I love seeing you
laughing a little
at my joke what was it
what does it matter this evening
never mind if I never find it
how many nights
have I wasted
not loving
my lonely head
swimming in air
just the head home
of the thoughts
as I write them
this evening
under the influence
of a loving mood

I love seeking advice
and then I love ignoring it
I love the sound
of the song
I'm being vague and I'm sorry
I go home
and alone in my room
try transmitting
popular songs
to your imagination
because you said
you're sad and lonely
they all disappear
I love ignoring it
this
is your song

I love with some sadness
even though it's amazing
the coffee in the morning
what it makes
happen to me
I stayed up too late
for sports from the West Coast
but it's a new day
and I'm looking at the forecast
and the West Coast box scores
other miracles technological and spiritual
I hope to find
I love with seriousness
when I love you
and take it seriously
when I make you coffee
in the morning
in the future
it's getting late
it's getting a little far away

I love how little love is
how meaningless
like open space
over the grass
over the grave
of an ancestor
a wild and troubled man you might be like
it is impossible to say how exactly or why
I love how the wind is changing
with the season
over this one last balmy day
an open space a box
you carry around

in relation
to the body
you carry the mind for it
around in the head
and it's the head I love
though it gets confusing
my thoughts
in my chest pocket
go on forever
like empty winter
a season big enough
for whatever thoughts one has within it
big enough to carry you
like a box
in the ground
freezing winter
all this time

I love like a tree stump must love the earth
and earth's moody liquid outer core
you let your legs
find a friend
far away
reach out and
a whole loving sequence
of stars and drawing the moon
on the sky extra large
singing on the sky drawing
the moon in light and trees in pencil
soft and fading
a powerful fucking
inside this
emotional tree stump
singing where the trees

dialing long distance
love loving
the whole comedy
I'm missing the friends
I've forgotten
this sentimental old commercial
reminded me how nice
to love and miss you
in the dark
through the telephone

I love the bad weather so long
gloominess gets into me
and I get into bad weather
trading punches
until I'm crying like a cloud
and I love the sun
as it goes away
after a while
it's killing me
down the road
in the space
between the visor
and the mirror
so I've learned to love
all kinds of weather
everywhere I've ever lived
various towns everywhere nondescript
wherever I've ever driven
going from one place to another
through glistening crazy ice
on the New Mexico highway
in the middle of winter
how long will I live

I don't know
the sun goes down
and the storm passes
eventually I don't know
how long I'll live
the nice ice yes
it is freezing
I love the most

I love
when I get practically killed by desire
thinking
I'll go into this sudden flame
a close intimacy
nevertheless I can stand it
amazingly sweet
signs and hints
you're laughing
you're in a dream
in the night
knocking on my door
I've been waiting for you
however you count
years or miles
tiny spacecraft
pinging back data
in obsolete code
you say love and I love
the idea of
I love laughing
and you're laughing
and I'm apologizing
for my thinking
getting practical

loving the fire or something
made of water
and letting off steam

I love that you can feel
it means all these things
for one
I'm sorry for saying love
without eye contact
directing my love
at tree branches and clouds
as if to say I love you and
please change me
moving world
but from my perspective
the world is still
a villain
for what is arbitrary
might be under control
and you're the light off the glass
of an office park
high above the highway
at sunset
with the suburbs
beyond what I can make out
of the forest
with not enough light yet
to really see you yet
in the animate world
you are none of that
for you have said all these things
I can remember
and being more like a building
I love you
your integrity

I love seeing you around
a corner on Main Street
the suddenness of love or realization
or the way everyone has
of explaining they knew they would faint
when they fainted
the time they discovered
the look they acquired
the time they met
the one they'd love
I love seeing you this way
not knowing you're in the exhale
between anticipations
coming around a corner
to find no air
a sheet of white sky
green hopeless grass
chairs with no seats
punchless pavement
not knowing where you are
I think I'll love you
at the end of time
when the maze
eases

I love the fog and the fear
and the way of the skull
and haphazard collections
and fighting for feeling
profound about animals
and knowing what the animal knows
what I could have been
in the midst of a walk
up a mountain

in the state of ascending
and noticing what I was feeling
that I love the fog
and coming out of revelation
what it feels like
in the intervening period
however long it is between
knowing I love you
and seeing you again

I love pitching and last night I lost
my perfect game
with two gone in the bottom of the ninth
and I was out there
on the mound
just thinking
I love the grass
and the dirt
the clean lines
it isn't the first time
I've told you about it
tonight at the observatory
you will be here tomorrow
baseball players have perfect names
from Darryl Strawberry
to Dick Pole
inscrutable words
through variegated time
and I want to tell you
my name comes to me
when you say it
the same physics
holds us together
anything is possible

but one outcome is
everything now

I love some words
they have sadness baked right in
in the moment
I can't find better ones
just trying
to say I'm just thinking
but think about that
when you say it
you mean feeling
I'm just feeling and thinking
this isn't the usual
autopilot
today is special
I take it on faith
and for the rest
of the death
of the soul
the sharkish world
takes advantage
like a storm
blows over
and when it is
not a storm
any longer
finds me in the words
making my plans
and so much for requests
so we move on
to the loneliness
in a photograph
the idea of you through fires

a pissed off soul
on a beach with the stupid seaweed and sunlight
idiotically glinting
off the water
looking like a million
pointless diamonds
I do not care for a second
but it passes
because of want
of company
a dreary feeling
and without counting
my friends
I grow tired
but it will blow over
as a storm
of plans
comes and finds me
in hibernation
a few months from now
I can see
my death blooming
in ways unforeseen
while greater forces
as in video games
press pause
and carry out
subsiding moods
of abject discomfort
and local responsibility
in sad harbors
where the ruins
of previous moods
are docked and waiting

I am not in the mood
though to retrieve them
I love some words
somewhat lonely requests
of places and farms
banks and dreams
and made plans
squinting a little
at the prismatic and enormous waters
where seabirds
are looking at me
gliding by
on a passenger ferry
like where the hell
does this joker
think he's going
the amazing sun
so large and dangerous
and decorative
and probably
unimportant right
right it's probably
at least in early usage
still working or rehearsing
not any final thing just yet
I love you
though the words
go on and on
and I know
I know
I know
I'll never find them
no matter how long
I look for them

the words are not words
they're me
in a different state
this dirge
painting air
over bones
and I am in a mood like paradise
singing to my own heart
whatever whatever it's okay it's okay
for there are others
there are others
who are restless
who are restless
and come find me again
when I am more myself again
and leaning
into the confidence
of new situations
waves
but not a boat
and not waves
just ocean
lapping the shore
when I am not the words again
but the version
of myself you love

I love a good question
it looks right at you
and when it is posed
that's when you know
you love
in the morning you're next to me
for once in my life

and I hold on
to your body
an extra minute
before both of us
go away
to make the coffee
and go to work
and you move
to a foreign place
where everything is oh
I love that extra minute
knowing even in the moment
the consequences
in future days
when I won't be able to recall
exactly what it was
keeping
me there
in the warm and nothing
vast air
and fragile current
a singular mood
it's not easy
I was just trying
to describe this
to a friend
but felt foolish
I was just watching
the World Series
and I want to tell you how
the best popular songs
the deepest drives
into October evenings
the most forlorn walks

through the woods
to some sunny beach
on the far end
of a cold lake
where I sit
scratching the word
weird
into sand
the color of the leaves
just before they fall
and not being certain
not feeling I'm myself
and everything else also
come to think of it
makes me miss you
and travel back
and it is weird
what I find
when I go there
because life is weird
lonely and connected
billions of years
what are you missing
who do you love

Confidence

Walk in the shade
and feel like that
part of morning
Missouri River
steam licked
by the light
of last night so what do you think
what else could these places have been
in earlier times
I'm not afraid
I never had
a sense of the moment
my face
looking at other faces
someone is dying
and when someone is dying
you understand
everyone dies
but this one person
is overwhelming
a minute the fabric takes
and I go on
feeling mediocre
most of the day is stupid
most of my
mood is sour
just now I felt
like I could

have had previous lives
but most of the time
I would have
to be stupid
but I have family
holding on
it is really the worst
to keep going
a carpenter
an engineer
no one understands
any part of
what the day presents
its fabric
but I am not
glad for the little
I have to do
just now
just a minute
that homesick clench
in my throat
the old feeling of feeling
sad the way it is
far from the grand
association you knew
who made you
who you are

Face like a train you said
face like some really good
sandwich while your
face moved
in a new apartment
all day like

the sun
Sunday morning
with the headache
that will probably continue
it all looks angry
from these big bus windows
a tropical storm
bearing down
on a friendly town
and everything
more apart
let's say you are right
there's nothing to worry about
walking and talking and
just doing the normal things
people are
grown-ups in constellation
every irrevocable face
like a computer screen
like a mirror looking
back is hard
life is there
just these phones
meals and premonitions

Just landed
in the quiet
a field my body is
the main thing
I want to get
rid of I suppose
these things
in my head
should come up

and see me
all tension
and big laughs
in the land of
wonder and mystery
is everyone the person
everyone wishes
everyone was
not tonight
not tonight
when I am wondering
what accountability
might make me
this dream where
I am a helicopter
looking for
a parking spot
coming out the other
side of some tunnel
sleeping through
the dark night
a reset for everything
going wrong in
dire days when
I was misadvised

The first word is mispronounced
and the rest are not much better
we are cheering
something obsolete
I guess
I love myself the most
a little miserable
drop of water

puts the sky
with the sea
that magic
is drastic I can't
say what remembers
me but I know
I don't
in confidence
get better
whispering in lieu of crying
I rifled through my books
for evidence
there was nothing
I understood
California where
I once lived
for a little
there was one
day of rain

The other day
I woke up and knew
my career was over
I think
you can say a lot
in a little space
but what would be
the point of
the long night's spool
unraveling small fears
continue to take me over
everyone can see
me and you
and everyone knows

I drank tea
and my head caved in
history
of the previous years of my life
gone and mostly wasted
but I wrote
these little things
and I could
let them go

Here we are
sunset in Boonville
Indiana things just
getting good
in my imagination
it's pretty
dire but always with me
the hope I'll live
again when
living gets quiet
around a lake
I don't get it
the car keeps going
so I do too
and accumulate ideas
I want to be
for you it's like
when you wake up
with a sore throat
you know what
is coming for
a couple minutes
it is really awful
but in whatever the day is

it begins to lose
its teeth and like
all horrors
eventually subsides
but not really
if your life has
been up to this point
about one thing
and tonight
is the last night
of whatever
your progeny
may recall you
in the sad sparks
of their choices
quiet nights
into the distance

Listen
this is a feeling
this is a feeling
and I have been
listening to it
you can buy all the votes
I'm a miracle
in the slow river
I can't make myself
care any more
where are we
going this
is a feeling
I'm giving it
time and place
midnight in

Acadia it is
cold and everywhere else
I've been and
the things I've been
reprise my
birthday April
in Paris what have
you done to
my heart

The morning comes to get you
it's ridiculous trying
to navigate the appointments
you need to keep
the body alive
while the body is
dying all the time
sometimes the world
reveals itself
unexpectedly you call
some large and
pointless corporation
and you get
answers
all of the sudden
an ankle has healed
but a back
and a knee go on
little issues
last night
I was
so much myself
I thought I might start crying
the body is the impossible burden of the body

too much the body too
much the body
I felt
around for
the light switch
and my head showed
my room to me
everything and everywhere
here I am
coffee I'm looking
at the back
of my hand and
yes I think
I know it
reasonably well

Today is the day
write it again
it goes away
I wrote this so
the moon landing
streak of starlight
twelve midnight
across the eyes
is that something
in the room here
with me hand
in my hand
there's no one
there or you
are again a pose
like my best
buddy tonight
I know if the

days go by too
fast we are stupid
discourse uttering
the politics again
and again coming away with nothing
special the coroner
reports oh well
heavy blanket just
me and you

What is this job
walking in the woods
it makes you feel
startlingly small
and before you know it
your life is
a mountain
scheduled out
six months in
advance a doctor
says ticking
time bomb over
and over again
and that's okay
that's reasonable
it's true for everyone
it is fall
and there is nothing you can do about it
I'm not going to wait
until I'm someone else
to start being myself it's fall
let's butter our toast
without prejudice or restraint
safe in the knowledge

that about health
there is nothing
we can shove
hands into
pockets it doesn't matter whose
go do what
you just did
but this time
do it better
by experiment
a prayer
we are different
and that is good
or I am
and I hear
the ghosts remarking
you are different
making plans all morning
and all evening breaking them
just to not leave
the house
sweet sunset
lights on all over
the uninterrupted town
there in the light
left on
I received a call
your family is having
trouble they said
and I just said oh
crap bacteria and
big smile
for the camera please
it is fall

and life is stupid
but I can be
stupider I can
in my great work
travel the country mile from
one eyeball to the next
and my heart
like an icebox
my wingspan
you're not ever what you were again
you're not ever what you could have been
let's keep
our appointments
with sleep
it's fall and we are
going to do
what we say

You already are
who you are
it happened in April
in the early 1980's
steam coming up
in a big field
invisible life
rotting invisibly
and now you could
be anywhere
and call me
and I would book a flight
I'm this coughing engine
I'm going to have
all these adventures
and tell anyone who will listen

that my life is beginning
that it began
that it happened
while I idled outside
unable to rain
I'm out here raining
six months six months
can you believe it
if you want to
don't close your eyes
everywhere you go
map the world

All things that happen request you
make a call
out of whatever
mind is remaining
it's raining
it's making me think
deft wind
what surprises
my body just keeps breathing
should I bring
pizza and beer
seeing as this is now
the most important thing
action taken
without much thought
I hardly know you
but I want your shoulder
what is meant by control nothing
important the most
important thing

The first instance
of the word September
there's a breeze
makes your mind sleepier
would it be wrong
to say the globe is tall
when it is wider than
but still taller than anything
even so
buy yourself
a world if you want
to have shitloads
of unfixable problems

If what you do
is who you are
will it make you happier
like a friend in your silent living room
a late night show
the best cloud
in the blue sky
the moon pulls water
no one should tell
another person explore
your future
it's the future
you can't explore it
your health breaks up
at your cute trying
hardly any time goes by
twenty years ago
well I guess
we knew all that
then didn't we

blue cloud
never stop joking
never stop saying
crazy random things

I just folded
a paper clip
into a satisfied
shape

I'm just joking
but I'm descended from whales
dreamy dreams I can't tell you
what I believe
in incommunicable revelation
and I need to go
get a haircut
I used to think
no one could know
anything but
I think I know
some things
and I'm the only one
so how's that
for confidence
best friend the
wilderness another
battle I have
little use for
and can't understand
this place
feels familiar to me
whatever it is I
can figure it out

working my way
out from under
these rocks hey
mystical cactus
the whole desert
the whooshing
wind in the empty
space

The good kind of sad
the good sad snuggling up
under the thought
that life is a sad face
in an old place
it could be better
but it's not
anywhere isn't
anywhere sadder
the whole confidence
you whisper like
a million dollars
words tumbling into
sentences rattling all night
the motherfucking
cages my family gathered
the artifacts of itself
our dread drawing a picture
of a house burning down
what was given
and what we took
good kind of
homesick
vigil
vigil
vigil

If I'm not in the text
with the next thing
I have no idea
what does that
billboard say
hello with scruples
hideaway in
the night of a highway
turnout bruised
food I'm getting down
on the coming years
but then you
suggest my presence
in the mood
of your sweeping
resignation I like
how happy your
unhappiness feels
I don't want to go to sleep
but to pay for this in the morning
like rain mostly water
so it's true you can
disappear not paying attention
you left
a window open
your carelessness
killed the animals
not the rising tide
you could have been
a reeling boat
a horrible period of transition
tiny lives in little mostly okay homes
welcome to the world
of suggestion
and carelessness

miracle after miracle
getting here at all

Whatever religion
I'd like to
believe it haphazardly
paying attention
almost not at all
through what you
said to the ends
of my fingertips
I'm going to have trouble saying this
but that light bulb impressed the day
I'm all kinds of slabs
of stupid steps
and stones a guy
who just really
only ever wanted
to get his coffee
outnumbered
in even the smallest conversation
video of the corn
out the window
I'm driving to the earthquake
doctor will I ever be neutral
about her
I probably will
how awful it is
to not feel awful
sleeping through the night

Here living under
certain fragrances
home town memory

for the birds
for the history
I missed not talking to you
for the past I can't say how many years
I was just a beard
in the kitchen
houses grow up
around these invisible
centers the kitchen
light all night
for the one time
you came over
chalk it up to timing
take all the power
in the megalopolis
pick out one light
through a town
you barely met
and miss

Hearing a door knock
in melting ice
in the freezer
a lack of ghosts
it gets boring
pouring gasoline
you are making connections
leaning a little
on the common
phrase once
in a while lifetime blue moon
I saw
the Red Sox
win it in 2004

I missed it
woke up trashed
on the floor in the living room
five in the morning
and talking
heads still at it
on television I thought
about how many
lights were on
in Fenway Park
a lightning flash
or geologic time
who cares
next time anything happens
I will have a better
television

In the heart machine
I know anything
can break
and stay broken
but swimming
in a pond
looking like glass
maybe that's reason
for optimism
but not about myself
my health
or what
if anyone
else reads this poem
or this other poem

I love a secret
not so much secret as quietly whispered

town to town
too long confidential
the secret part
of larger secrets
sleeping from one
sentence to another
wonderful secret
meetings in the belly
where I might
have felt not seas
not exactly
but waves
maybe moods
deaths in dresser drawers
locked out of disclosure
no secret breathing
planet golden golden
secret thoughts
confidential hours standing
still looking out
the window in case
anything happens
when anything happens
go on in secret
everything coming after
you go on
in secret wherever
you are you are
and when anything
happens that's when
you happen

I have to look
and the window
is there

soft light
what do you think
pretty much just
sheep out there
saying we demand
a voice in television
to gather up
and bring the state
of the art
to our level
so what say
the candidates
in total depravity
I'm keeping open
my mind beyond
business hours
every decision
put me here
genuflection
precipice paint
a little picture
of me gazing
out to you
on the cliffs
of an island
last night
the stairs seemed
silly as we chatted
I wanted to talk
to you forever
but I put on
my shoes if
I look at my closed
bedroom door

and I have
a little light
on wherever you are
will the gravity
of my thinking
about you pull
you into loud and sustained
prehistoric orbit at least
indescribable
delicate lizard
sunning on a rock
I can't touch
all of your displacement

Let's say a truth
and walk around
the big pond the forest
and truth in the
sandwich I am
going to have
to be honest
probably before lunchtime
and be impossible
most of the morning
my mood sucks
where were you
when I was drunk
and charming though
of course but I am
realizing I leave
not enough
empty space
empty is in empathy
as I am into

ice floes satellite
data what we send
out and what comes
back to us
thirty thousand feet
of possible elevation
this squeaking and crackling record
love songs in times that were difficult
someone in the world might know
exactly what you want
how to talk
to your body
like this whisper
like this second
drunk in a garden
of all the animals
and violent combinations
that I was
for these years
this one who is
impulsively walking
into traffic
to cross the street
to get to you

Something else is
exclamation oh
indecipherable true
praise oh and what
is on the other
side of that wall
but honest and
transparent doubt
I doubt my choices

oh they were
grammatical gravity
I gave up
ghosts and God
is good when
I read out loud
call back
the generations
another cup of
coffee sitting down
to late lunch
late life on a fastball
passed down
father to son
in the nursing home
late at night
in the hospital
when the lights
go down you fall
in love with walking
it's confusing
having to learn
to die or travel
the miles of breathing
to get to death
I got this great
advice from a hospice
nurse look just
look that's it look
does the face look
uncomfortable or at
peace uncompromising
aspect the moon
shining on it

through the window
nurses gliding ghosts
out there
in the hallway
I never dreamed
I was an advocate
like what is
the downside
to more morphine
at a certain point
the arrangements
you've made irrelevant
2012 oh Summer
Olympics these distant
connections hearing Hava
Negilah perfect
gymnastics of crying
which happens
alone in the car
all the time anyway
while we keep growing
up until we don't
hear the synthetic sounds
anymore just
bird songs
the awful morning after
life's not so bad
which is horrible
and oh warble
and stutter nothing
no higher praise
than indifference

Calling into the earth
does not happen

on the telephone
if it's raining
it's raining all day
and everything else
is forgotten
forgiven for what
can you do when
the quote won't close
there's a door
and another
world on the other
side so much
then for consolation
for it was
a rainy day charged
and foolish
and should I write
to you
a letter
my magnet
somehow a billion
thoughts together
the word together
going through
going through going
through the things
one says

Babies understand
our angry computers
this morning
the world was different
did you notice
that when I was famous
I was reeling from the fame

I couldn't walk
down the street forget about public bathrooms
God what is the worst thing
I could have done this morning and oh shit
did I do it
I go into holes in the ground
because the king
of the seeds is the king of the world
but let's say
you went away
for the weekend
and when you came back
a band played
all the trees
were gone
a sad old song
menacing faces
up in the catwalk
of an abandoned arena
in my imagination
I have a brick from there
I'll put it in my tomb
I'm naming
my unborn son
pilgrim dusk
on the big river
my friends
all royalty
don't tell
anyone

A big tear
in the sky
if I could switch

off the river
at night
I could sleep
out of all the faces
the coastline
out of many of us
we find ourselves
unable to run
in dreams
on all the charts
facing sorry
attrition I felt
sorry had a simple
name academic
in the dark
the plug
a little lamp behind
my television
when you visit stay
with you
all night

I'm loving the hallway
out loud at night
to say nothing
to the only mirror
in my apartment
America's loving
the bats
after the bugs
it's dusk I guess
I want to say
back to you
whatever you said

to stand over a river
on a bridge and watch
the water and
I want to see it
and dream you
are next to me dreaming a full moon
linked in the complex
of constellations
of influence
and many harbors
and docks where
I watch activity
my frame of mind
alights and goes
to Canada in the
manner of a bald
eagle how even
friendly borders
are very serious
and I am
but I joke about it
and when you reach
for me I don't
believe it and you
know about it
and anywhere is
better than that

I found nothing
every time I looked
under the floor
into the deep
foundation of
the house which

fit me snuggly
but is always
bending around
the lines
on my hands
my whole life
something happens
and I worry
about it until
I go to sleep
and blanket the dark inside
altogether ingenious
and other reasons
at the top
of a mountain
to be so out
of breath and say
to yourself
what is this noise
pounding in my head
oh my God
it's my heart
and my ship then
out to sea
out of sight of land
big freedom
like a prison go on
and explain to me
that you were not
real at all
as true a line
as a bird flies
that here is my
indecision and the fact

of being alone
your friends
you haven't talked to
in so long
there will be gigantic spirits to receive us
you say I don't believe you
and I don't

The wind moved
the door and walked
into the room
it was excited for beer
it was late in the evening
of giddy restraint
I was talking
out of what I want
there's no imagination
I will probably just think
should I cut off my beard all day
and John and I decided
we like being bored so
you could argue
that's not boredom
you have something
and someone wants
to take it away
from you someone
goes around screaming
someone stole my phone and I need it
my heart
is someone else
someplace pretty
different because
the formal structure

of this poem and
my thoughts are more uniform
our friends have families now
they go on forever
I keep thinking
I've done nothing but it's not true
I can't say it's wrong either
great boredom under
every infinite series John

When my fate expires
in other words
I'll know
how I've been speaking
my whole life
in the wrong
language in a city
I saw once
in a dream
it was my birthday
and I was old
like an old rocket
and cognizant of blood
in my hands and
sand in my toes
I keep trying to say
good morning
to silence and light
it's just
I will miss you
the water called back
and I was saying how
I was just wondering I'm
squeezing your hand

too much
to just say
I'm doing fine

I heard an old song
say carry on
it's how I get
to know you
I get that way
in the manner
of tall buildings
in the way of construction
they've got the whole country
hooked up to
EKGs tonight
the few of us who have
gone off-script
into personality
uncultivated
since we were young
and when we were
very young we were
love songs in the
stars cool water
humming Stand
by Your Man
to ourselves
how bright
under the moon
the snow is

And if my name
boarded a great ship
pale ghost reanimate

the ocean
I think about
has all these islands
and is so emotional
waiting here for you
to tell me
I'm okay
circling around
the city where
we are living
this land's cursed
since the first
exclamation
when the animals
got real quiet
and I can hear
what I hear
when the windows
are closed
don't look back
on your life
I had a chance
and missed it now
I'm okay though when
I want to love you
otherwise I shut up in here
more of the world
and missed and
had and missed

And it's dark
and that's when
we're at our most
familiar

it's quiet
but there's a storm
lumbering around
our whole region
my God is smoking
an ocean
this darkness should see us
from the mask to the inside world
I felt I was going
to look back
from now on to mark the day
my life began
the day I started writing
I started fading
looking back through hard times
under the trees
and snowing about it
getting old and telling
everyone about it

Unafraid
the house is full
of noises
the world of clouds
whatever word
you whisper in my ear
I wonder when
the sky rips apart
if I then
hold it all
in my head
at the same time
it's a little like
real life

it's blue like
purple hell
the back of your hand
here in the service
and on the way
to work this morning
all the photographs
I had a memory
I told the dream
keep dreaming
I'm trying to work
okay I'm getting up
you keep sleeping
it's why
I like to chat
with doctors
and you know how
there is this feeling
taken care of

You remember whatever
you remember how late it is
to wake up soon
the world too much is too much a whale
they pack you
on a boat
look how we're
sardines and pretty
happy about it
most of the time
both feet in the game
I let up
and let you win
I didn't want to lose

but I didn't want to play anymore
and now we're talking
we're hanging out
seeing each other
in our best moves
don't go
don't keep moving west forever
you can't live in the ocean
thousands of years
now I remember
it was my mom saying
boychik why do you
assume the worst
all the time
you are going
to be okay
I have no proof
but you are

Whatever you said
in the past
it doesn't mean
you can't change
your mind again
there's no time
I'm going
to a new city
to be a force
in the breakup
of the most ice
and like a diamond
in the sky
every major age
someone was you
the way you are

and navigating
empty winter roads
being baffled
breaks me up come
down the stairs
where the car is running
who you are is my audience
in the story we are
all these mornings we don't acknowledge
I wanted to wait until life
started and then life started
I'm sorry
you know I'm
just thinking

You are a tree
in a soft breeze
I'm sorry you passed out back there
the strings
started to swell
we drove
past this elk
on the top
of a hill
it will be millions of planets when I die
I want to crash my car into outer space
the ocean doesn't go here
but here it is
and no one knows anything
except they love
and are troubled

And if it feels good I'm wondering
what's good what's good out there
people in the air

I'm really asking you
there's a lot going on
in a number of associations
and saying you did but really you did not
do all this stuff
so I'm shifting my thoughts
into long rows
and whatever I'm doing with my hands
I'm probably going
to keep on doing
more words
more words
man now I'm
in the drug
store and the light
outside of night
the wreckage in my head
humbling

And if the water
coming down
is talking you say
well now
I guess it
is all over

My heart is beating
trying to decide
what it means
it's like a hammer
my best guess is travel
do I have the means
rolling stone
Thanksgiving coming up

my family is bored
who can we bring
into our sphere of sad dysfunction
making it through the day listening to
I don't care for the president
sure I respect the office
what are you putting on the line
your poetry
proprietary and
like music
you want it to say
about you
if the water coming down is talking
go up to it
hey what's up water
filling the container
a reminder
I'm a little
buzzed too early in the evening
how unaware
I am in the light reading
is this an attribute
a tendency
what what
no really what
and I go
make a little money
and if I lose it
oh I lost it

I don't think I'm going to die today
but if I did
the living me
would feel incomplete

what is happening
to us in the living room
I'm going out on a limb
and saying this
is not enough
it isn't enough
to know I could feel complete
dying some other day
I disagree
on knowable facts
but it feels like there is decency
I'm glad it's calming down
in the world in the aftermath
of a big storm
can we be overwhelmed together
a snowstorm
made me stay
where I was
I spent the night
in a weird hotel
near the Chicago airport
I kept thinking if you were here
if you were here
but I'm not myself
with you around
I slept
for three hours
there was a shuttle
back to the airport
it's the most boring
of worlds unless
you are crying right
and because of everything you gave me

I know there is
all this stuff
I want to tell you
because I won't

Breakwater

And then so what
about dreams I'm learning
past fear
abstract sickness
the most vital
materials
are a kind of inner
a whistling kind of
inner phenomenon

I hope I sound a little like hope
making out
a living honey
I want you
a little
to say how
I feel

You point out
the best things
and I see them
what are colors
in the first place
forget it I want the song
to say the daylight
coming on
can worry no matter
how wasted

the explicit feeling
of being the way you are
always going on
in the space
around you

The past collapses
you are waiting
for something
what is it
for something to come
the size
of what is
viewing us

Fifty caterpillar heads
in nature

I'm more
transcriber than anything
else mimics irrational
voices I came
west before the erection of towers
it's all in flux
I'm shocked
an object seeking lightning
anything can happen
to this art

Get rid of it
all afternoon
the lives a train could take
you away from
not bread

but something
I love you
be happy
I don't know
I'm gullible so
I'll stop
a stone
eruption
a thousand years
there's bread and all these columns
on the ground reuniting
the party was fun
I'll see you
it's no good
see you later

And in the background
the city went suffering
you could be patron saint of artless sincerity
political
and nobody feels anything
I want a romance celebrating fear of estrangement
I go around the triptych
there are better ways
of telling stories
my friend I am
my society pronounced something new
I made it
I was the king and
everything isn't good and
it is my fault disaster
nuclei breaking down
this ground floor
this time keeps going

But light dictated the rules
I saw my friends
it's not that I want to
redo lying on the bed
I go wild
for dimness
when you fall
in love the grand
pattern set forth
in the cathedral
is everything
innovative
wait hold on
to focus I say
thanks cartoon cloud
it's cold and raining
it has a classical ring
you teach me something
and we deal
the cards back
and forth
basically
forever

Bitter flavor
however many faces I have
no doubt I am looking into the real thing
there's a blot
of ink that looked at me
a bolt of lightning
look at me
baby animals
psychiatry
if I have anything strange
let it be my face

congregation
today your faces
are full and link us

I think what
something else thinks
of me matters
me and the gulf
stream roll my
need is most
astounding it matters
but it doesn't really matter
all that much

And I stood facing
the same progression
all over again
the film
the room
lights
the screen
got dark
the street
half a century
of lunar aspiration
our only chance
to touch
I carried my breath into the phone
I sat alone
in my room
and called you

Go on
open all the books
take a high arc

step back jump shot
words don't have words for this
ten seconds ten minutes
the heart curves
or it floats
your life
is gonna get weird
dribble out the clock
take a breath
and miss it
I miss it

This is the year
a little slower
a little steadier
it's sad like a party
on the other side of glass
out in the woods
the devil is out
in the woods and the library
studies my thoughts
the monologue I don't
actually say June was
the only word
for the size
of the street
when your body
has doubled and tripled
I am fluent
here solid
and bright

I hush
it lets me keep going

no illuminating
charts and numbers
it's too late
your lifetime
I was so whatever that I hid
it all means shit to me
breakfast
the window
the water
you're saying more than you can
that's reputation
there's the woods
be a pilot of the living
false front
in the dark
stand by me
just you for a million years
unflagging true religion
it's just us
between
home
and
the war

And it was really good and bad
and it was nobody
and nobody's songs
and the food was
sunning itself on the rocks
an hour at a time
waiting and knowing
I can wait like this forever
it'll be raining
and you will call

my name quietly
but I can't hear you

I had to let go of my Sputnik
a long time ago
decades
and now this adult thing
epithalamion slow-cooker laughing
in the back yard
and I'd like to go back there
and be a little better
to have the evidence
in your diary
that I was good
when we were young
friends
are having
babies
and singing them to sleep
we're seeds
I'm sick of the worthless
body
more beautiful than stalks of corn
highway wildflowers
you're in the back seat
looking at the stars

Lips turn words
into transgressions
this one is hard to say
on good days
good people are raw
they have a little nothing
they share it for once

I am the light
from the windows
filling the room
I love you
your business is my business
it's a threshold
a coast
the ocean
did you see the shark out there
did I see the shark
what am I doing
in the water

Let it be true
that I saw you
astonishingly
there after
the big one ended
all streaks are amazing
all on their way out
our little disagreements
press on
us we carry them sufficiently
they make up our disposition
we carry them
mostly without blame
the big one
the big one can be
anything it's spring
training it's
still the previews I forgot
what movie it's still early
in some war I'm saying
there's all this

hope still and sometimes
it's so long
so long my love knowing
what the odds are tonight
I'm getting out
of baseball

I don't want to be different
but the years fly by
Boston
I'm coming home
to mend
along the line of the railroad
years are simply irrational
it's years
I never see
it's life
it's for somebody
I used to know
to go into
my agitation
to go in for looking
never helps I don't
remember when I think
back on it
my teammates
my career either long
and illustrious though
it may well have been

In the winter
and longer
a trick of the eye
and piety forever

the size of the heron's memory
I am offended
there's a stiff
mercy I'm not
supposed to possess

A worrisome invitation shining
history burying itself
in skin and chemicals
in the eyes
prior to the patent you are
a new type
of design whatever it was
I was discussing with you
to get it clear
I knew things
were misplaced
a little brush
with being alive
I'm with dreams
I'll gently manage
my love
horns now
and flutes begin
screaming now

It rained most of the night
we go on
past necessary
and for the rest of the continent
my imagination runs into trouble
I'm gonna wait right
here until the captain
comes back

in disappointed
dispatch all these
dumb flags and emblems
I mean to know whether
I have forgotten
anything
it rained
and the rain
sustained it
under skies
of permanent danger

Ascension
behaving like the bed
of a river or the head
of an island
it rained
most of the night
whiskey drunk in the air
I am beginning
to miss
it's raining and the paths
are muddied
I mean together
if I am beginning
to understand please
advise

Do you believe these clouds
there's no answer
I believe
in the devil
god in the sky
everything I've done

just one way of doing
things I seem
to be real to divide
and to carry
it's the middle of winter
it's cold outside

I stopped drumming my fingers
on the arm of the chair
I thought about reference
I faced the earliest sunrise in America
the security of definition
however temporary
every morning I think
I have to get
out of here
and climb
out of bed
driftwood
fragrance
the white noise of the air conditioner
and I remember midnight
anxiety and finally regard
myself a problematic
blood
rushing to the head
the gravity disaster
progressing into audience
sentimental
and intolerable

It's just shelter
the summer
doesn't need you

I just thought of that
when you go downstairs
in the morning
and everyone is there you
are working
a foremost citizen
at one with Massachusetts
we don't know
what's out there breathing
and sounding we don't
we just don't
there's no proof
no smudge of starlight
streak on the car window
we all drove
a hundred miles an hour
while everyone slept

There was a noise
in the other room last night
I thought I heard someone
whispering to me
make a list of everything
you didn't just forget after a couple days
your cells
it's quiet
I invented them
I wrote something I wanted to live in
it's the closest
I can get
stuttering family
friends there was
a noise in the other
room

I could get to
where I feel
confident a succession
of early hours
a stupid day
a monstrous night
I wake up in and walk
around a little
you work really hard
and lose in the championship game
and spend your life attending
an endless succession
of banquets the words
just pile up
there's a scramble and then
it's over
the unenviable task
of getting up in the morning
but your dreams
stay stellar
and what lightning
is hot enough
to do is irrational
photos of you when you were young

Cut to the sun
a sign says beware
but what are you supposed to do
to be alone in the face
of some natural
disaster you are
all the houses
you've lived in
you are in a movie

quiet now
you are in a
movie everyone is
trying to kill you
now go on
that way
forever

Please
you have to wonder
what is the little you have
the lake sitting like a pearl
in the middle
of suburban whatever it's a dream
my dog is still here
it's a dream
the blinds closed
and no one cares
about seeing you anyway
it's a dream
we're on time
we're drunk
and leaving our cars wherever this isn't
my wedding
speech to you
we say hold on
a minute we're
helping each other
I don't know why we have other people
it's not for breathing
it's not that kind of essential
it's a dream for which we have
these biological reasons
other people
please

join us
on behalf of everyone
who is here
whoever you are
holding
me up and I am
here to say I am
always talking with you

And let us say that
what I wanted
was to be here
for a long time
it's very late
and I'm up
writing it
needs to happen
I thought you were
in my head
even when I had to look
for you elsewhere
I thought you were
in my head
and the years passed
and you weren't
anyway when you grow up
you turn
your address
to the bigger world
you can't
simplify

If I'm different
another year's gone
so long year

if I leave
another tomorrow
the mushy background
over the shoulder
a hundred years
is no good reason
you're sad I'm sad it's the only
reason
forever whatever
you do
you did

In the kitchen
in the middle
of the night I was
thinking about relentlessness
there's no good reason
I was there
and there was proof
my life was real
the wilderness frowned
I surrounded myself
with crazy people
and loved them very much
my hand
can't really know what
my heart did except
it does know
think about it
you relentlessly dream
a habitat
it would be better in there
are you better
are you here in here with me

It's true
it's right there
kind of hiding
kind of pausing
outside in a rainstorm
it's the door of the one I love
and I'm waiting there
until the world makes known its horrible preference
or I'm eating a bagel
in a coffee place
and "Cleaning Windows"
by Van Morrison
comes on the
radio and no one
who isn't me
knows I was just thinking
when I was little
my street was big
and there is so much
I have
a lot to learn

You can keep throwing faces on
it won't keep
all day
from beaming back at you
sky I like the shade
to be far from the lilacs
and near me
mourning doves getting bolder
just hanging around
they are the ones
when I tap the window who
remain I have to return

something to the store
I have to keep living here
for the rest
of my life
my hat needs
a new hat
our frightening
long flirtation
curtains
I can't leave the house
the road will not suit me
I have to keep being this person
you might like
these
are all the good
ideas

You criticize without
really making
a jewel in a pool
sunlight won't
warm up
look it's the loud time of year
the part of the year
when it is over
you will look back on
and wonder how you survived
I think it was inertia
you had an idea
it could have been anything
and it must have sustained you
like visiting the sick
and dying part of it
is self-serving

I choose to think of it that way
the birds flying
around whatever God is
and the light
hits another thing
just right
and doesn't say
all the years
you can waste
on being alone

Whatever hears us
running the faucet alone in the kitchen
can make you
a little cliff
sunning
not far from here
a view
upon a stadium
a mall where I have hibernated
I come out of it feeling nostalgic
but missed
nothing major
the problem is knowing where to start
you start and the ending
is in sight

There there I know I know
no place
is a strange world
the universe
could still be there please
still be
what I was

afraid of
circles before the earth
the frame you find
you fail to understand
where was that highway where a landscape
happened
to make me go on
I can't say what is in my heart
is unselfish sometimes
out here with my allergies
under the stars
there's too much
light I thought I was
the difference
between the light
and the dark
moment of another
world singing
alone in the car
but I am not
moving this thing

You are the one
for me you are
the one I can't think about
it has been years
longer than
The Civil War
and longer than it has
taken the world
to change
I got up today
thinking about
an ultrasound

general transmissions
I got up thinking
this world is getting me down
and the uniqueness of sound
in the middle
of the night
I wanted you
to hear my head
a little buzzing
some tiny thought in orbit
its own dark
manipulation
of the surrounding
every day
of your life
the same everything
is falling into
an amazing center
we don't know who
it is you
or else you are
someone else

As a kid you are not
a light bulb burning
or the stuff you sing with
the radio you are
whatever is nothing
but the feeling
of feeling it
from the top of the stairs
you hear the crowd
on the television
some big thing down there

shining and fierce
the living room
when it's over
you are so sad
a million years could not fix it
and you remember
and you remember
you remember

Sometimes
I hated what I liked
if it was the truth
I would make a list
pros and cons
and only
list the pros
sometimes is not specific
I know but where
does the map go
the feeling you are
the one true thing
of tired life
always over
and above
what you think
or you want

You are not ever what you thought
you are not what the news says
you are happening
you are so much better
than you used to be
you used to be
the great magician

do we stand for the body
do we stand for the mind
when we die
who will save us seats
the best anyone
says about me
is I am among
the living
investigation

I can't sleep here tonight
just waking up again shouldering the big
surface of light
but everything is off
and it is so quiet
okay it was a long day
long year
I admit it

It's enough
that you did something
on this impossibly
pristine day
are you ready
to deliver anything
worth anticipation
that's the shine
of your mistakes
lighting up the ocean
whoa is
that a beach down there
is that your bed
the smoking sky I celebrate
the worst thing

twice it's enough
to wake up a little damaged
so why make up
a different survival of
ancestors who were abolitionists
waking up
every morning just
praying you
make good choices
in our dreams we help each other
we carry these ancient
artifacts carry each
other and
we're young

It's like driving a small thought into the ground
a small thought but a good one
a little light
just for you
off the shining face
of a living creature

Stop crying
the winged seeds
of cedar trees
the same paralysis
the raining face of your apartment
I'm not ready for this
tonight my talking across
even the softest
iron snow

I know
I'm here trying

to make this
exclamation point
a little quieter
trying and failing
to be a message
over the trees
a breeze that reaches
the house for a minute
to be better than
the same old thing you want
me to say I won't
be a problem
but I am
and it is
difficult
here are the numbers
I'm seeing
from some elevation
a great chart
confusing
and subject to whatever is out there
governing us
creepy and brutal spirit
listen it is what
is around your house
ink in your pen
when I see you
I'm misplaced
a plant a wildflower
unidentified flying nothing
a parabola or
this whole
comedy thing

For what just keeps going
I tried to make sense
for a little while
I did
look out
I'm a stranger mostly
and everyone loves a stranger
a little
from a distance
and with a lot of reluctance
a little fear
something manmade in the middle
of nature
these trees not here fifty years ago
in the rain
in the traffic
I tried to be a stranger
and everyone remained familiar
a new personality
growing out
splashing around

I just remembered
to say it
the way I'd say it
I'm holding the big
edge of distraction
trying to not
let it fall away
trying to be a little stupider
really magnificent life

I'm so tired I'm lying
but then this town waits
a second for me

post office and bank
I like other people's
obscure and rolling luck

I wish I could stop
and today I do
you can stay
with this water
splashing sun
you can come in
do the right thing right
don't worry
characterize gently
it's all ready
this time
okay
so what was yesterday
a lot got done
I thought
about you
and now you're here

And if you are going
to make it you might
as well make everything
I would like to test it
but what the hell could stand up
to that kind of scrutiny
the tiny taxpayer in me
has no idea
what time is it
twenty years ago
what is inside
the sandwich

from now on this is where I live
and every day is
not like this

I can see a line
where one thing
makes another thing
make a sound
and moves the plot
around and makes us
feel we have
to say something
it's compulsive
your items are looking
at you and their faces
are not kind
car headlights the toaster
that tree in the yard
has so many arms
it doesn't do much
the wind takes
the sound and goes
to the next place
your life
in the middle
of all these other
lives you remember when the telephone
would ring when you hoped it would

Grass and breeze
how can I be
and what am I going to know
these are good mottos
facing the national bird

facing hypochondria
grass and anxious breeze
we do not want to be
where mosquitos are
we are who we are
and we just
want the truth

I held my breath in the future
why am I terrible
is what the music says
in flight up
in the map of the world
in the future
I'm orbiting this
great joy I deserve

And eventually that lint
on your shirt
is in the midst of
all this landscaping
I saw one leaf
doing its thing
in the wind
while the others
just sat there
give it space
leave the fireworks to the crew
out on the lake
just watch
it happen and let the right time be
the right time
I like that you keep talking
even when you notice

I'm not
saying anything at all

I was perfect or thinking
about responsibility
the sun
getting lighter on me
retrieval of what I lost in dying
one day at a time you said
I would like
to write the history of perfection
all night
moonlight through living
room windows
through nerves
leaves of just this
season of perfect
green influence

Tidying up the house
in memory of
my love for
the dying fragment
a little dust in the corners
the work of dying
and what it takes
are you the hospital
the whole cemetery
the day was dying
so we watched it

It's a dream
this is my life
a little lens you have to peel

off the water
a way of looking great
for posterity
my fear of the movies
my fear welling up
where am I going
in the middle
of the universe
you are not
what you might
have guessed

In like two seconds
you decide either
you like it or not whatever
it is a shivering break
in the crust
a gorge into
the deep shit of the world
the light
arrives
and I raise up
one stupid finger
to say
yes
here I am

But where will I
be when I know
where I'll live
whatever I wanted
the most
happened
hours ago

this mail-boat
the first
best thought
I want to be
where no one is
for you to
surprise me there

Straight up
the sky straight
down the ground
I'm the strangest
ratio
well we all are

From strange ropes
the sky what
did I learn
from this language
all night
from the light
I kept waking up
in the television kept
yawning and turning
over fitful restless
I left I wrote we are
the love of just who we are out here
shooting around in
the center of
the night
what can you learn
and when can you sleep

Would you rather
be an animal
well then pay
attention life is mostly
experience you realize
you believe what
you realize you
believe but I just
think about driving
rain a storm
an animal behind
the wheel of my car

The radio can't understand
the shower I can't
understand why
I would want
to wake up
I'm up
between today and technology
and go bake a little
in the sun
the summer is terrible
all year I'm waiting save a couple weeks
in the fall
they save me
the radio gets good

A house is a machine
nothing in the ocean
at night
nothing in the world not done
I need sleep

but there's no lock no key
there's no sleep
and I need a world
and the world half-starts
in dinosaur eggs
a perfect little
obstacle of proof
obstacle of proof
the distortions
we fall in love
if we can remember
if we are happy
dealing out
our lives
or without
our lives
live forever

Apologize to everybody every day
for whatever you have done
for the rest apologizing might provide
the release of
guilt for the fact
of saying
the words
out loud
passing the food
without saying a word
just staring
at the TV while
answering questions
genuine and lackadaisical
in nature
what do we have that's deserved

these whizzing lights
in a city of forgiveness

All the things
I know I know
there are no holes in that knowledge
there is a disaster
and there is no need
to avert it
there is a concert
a garden a museum
a heron
some people die before
the new Bob Dylan
album is released
and after
we are gone
we are gone
over and over
again and on
and after
we are
we were
forever

You might not know
you might know
you are dying
a hand on your head
and you walk
in the other room
you make the most of it
and stay in there listening
to voices really far away

who knows
who knows you here
it's quiet
and what are you building a bridge
to get back to being
something I remember
I don't remember
it's confusing
saying hello
to pictures
or being gentle
placing a rock on a rock
and walking into another room
your hand on your head
another room and another

Come back
life knows you
and the river
and the mosquitos
up to the top of your head
in high elevation
the slow courtesy
to remember we were humans
the invention of flight
the first sentence stretching out a little
but still sleeping
through the wave
an incredibly lovely hand
a city that doesn't feel
like home yet
in the purple sky
and all this buzzing
and whirring

I refuse
to accept eternal
sounds make
me seasick
to come back
and
all is forgiven
to wheel around
and see you again

Acknowledgements

Thanks to the editors of the following journals who published these poems, sometimes in a different version: *Incessant Pipe, Robot Melon, Spoke too Soon, SpringGun,* and *Verse.*

Thanks to Sarah Pessin, Eleni Sikelianos, Bin Ramke, and Brian Kiteley for your insightful, generous reading of a previous version of this manuscript.

Thanks to all the friends who looked at it, listened to it, and told me what you thought. Thanks to my family, and thanks to my friends who are also family. I really love you guys.

Thanks to Joe and Sam at Brooklyn Arts Press for all of your help turning these poems into a book.

And thanks, finally, to Broc Rossell for all of the work you did editing this book. You helped me say what I was saying.

About the Author

Seth Landman is the author of four chapbooks and the full-length poetry collection *Sign You Were Mistaken* (Factory Hollow Press, 2013). His work can be found in *Boston Review, io, Jellyfish, Lit, Forklift, Ohio* and elsewhere. He received his PhD in Creative Writing and Literature from the University of Denver (2013) and an MFA from the University of Massachusetts (2008) where he is currently an Academic Advisor.